JOHN OSTEEN

THE
BELIEVER'S
#1
NEED

BOOKS BY JOHN OSTEEN

The Confessions of a Baptist Preacher
Reigning in Life as a King
How to Claim the Benefits of the Will*
How to Demonstrate Satan's Defeat
How to Flow in the Super Super Natural
How to Release the Power of God
Pulling Down Strongholds*
Rivers of Living Water
The Believer's #1 Need
The Bible Way to Spiritual Power
The Divine Flow*
The 6th Sense . . . Faith*
The Truth Shall Set You Free
There is a Miracle in Your Mouth*
This Awakening Generation
What to Do When the Tempter Comes
You Can Change Your Destiny
A Place Called There
Four Principles in Receiving from God
How to Minister Healing to the Sick
Keep What God Gives
Love & Marriage
Receive the Holy Spirit
Saturday's Coming
ABC's of Faith
What to Do When Nothing Seems to Work

*Also available in Spanish.

Order from:
John Osteen Publications
P. O. Box 23117
Houston, Texas 77228

(or from your local Christian Bookstore)

ISBN 0-912631-09-0   A John Osteen Publication

THE BELIEVER'S #1 NEED

A few years ago, after there had been a mighty out-pouring of the Holy Spirit in our denominational church, we were busy reaching out in every area to spread the Gospel. During those days, we had a service at the downtown rescue mission. A group of the deacons in our church went with me for this service. One of them decided to invite a local denominational preacher to go along and preach the message that night. We were all so full of the Holy Ghost and joy we could hardly wait for the service. The brother who was going to do the preaching did not know what to think of our excitement.

When we arrived, we went to a back room to have a prayer meeting. This prayer meeting turned out to be very unusual. Each one of us prayed in turn while the others praised the Lord and agreed. It seemed like heaven came down as we all confessed who we were in Christ and our victory over the devil and demons. We rejoiced because people would be saved and delivered in the service that night.

The man we had invited to preach that night was the last one to pray. All of our praying was strange to him. I am not criticizing his praying; however, I am simply reporting on what happened. Here is how he prayed:

"Oh, God, you know what a weak worm of the dust I am. You know, Lord, that I am weak and unworthy. You know, Lord, that I am a failure. Oh, God, I am such a black-hearted sinner! Oh, Lord, I am so weak and unworthy. Help me!

Help me! Help me! Oh, Lord, how can you use such a sinner as I am.

As I listened to him pray, I wondered if instead of getting him to preach, we should try to get him saved!

He went ahead and preached that night and did his best, under the circumstances. Of course, we all backed him up in prayer and trusted God to reach the people. After the service, I met with him over at the right side of the building and began to talk with him. I asked him, "Brother, are you really in the shape that you talked to God about when you prayed?"

He asked, "What do you mean?"

I said, "Well, you told God that you were a great sinner, weak, unworthy, black-hearted and a failure. Now, I want to know if you are really in that condition?"

"Oh, Brother Osteen, you know what I mean."

I said, "I guess you meant what you said, unless you were lying to God. Let me quote you a scripture and then ask you a question. The Bible says in I John 1:9, 'If we confess our sins, He is faithful and just to forgive us our sins, and to cleanse us from all unrighteousness.' The question that I want to ask you is this: What do the letters A-L-L- spell?"

He said, "All."

I said again, "What do the letters A-L-L- spell?"

He replied, "All!"

The third time I asked him, "What do the letters A-L-L- spell?"

Frustrated, he began to reply, "It spells .... Oh, I see, that does make a difference, doesn't it?"

"Yes, Brother, the Blood of Jesus Christ has cleansed you from *ALL* unrighteousness, and if you

2

are cleansed from *ALL* unrighteousness, then you are not a worm in the dust, a failure, nor a black-hearted sinner. If you are cleansed from *ALL* unrighteousness, then you can stand tall in the presence of God without inferiority and in the presence of the devil without fear."

This story illustrates what this book is all about. A great number of Christian people live under condemnation and a sense of weakness and inferiority. The Body of Christ should move in scriptural authority, but there will never be that authority as long as there prevails a sense of inferiority.

The truths in this book are to strengthen, encourage, and enlighten you as to how you can come out of a cringing, cowardly attitude to become a stalwart soldier for Jesus.

The devil knows that his time is short.

God is unveiling Bible truths in order that there will arise a body of people who will walk in righteousness and shatter the kingdoms of darkness!

The Book of First John speaks of two kinds of people on the earth — the children of the devil and the children of God. (I John 5:18-19)

II Corinthians 5:17 says, "Therefore if any man be in Christ, he is a new creature: old things are passed away; behold, all things are become new."

WE ARE NEW CREATURES!

Let's look at how God sees this new creature. The Apostle Paul said in Romans 1:16&17, "I am not ashamed of the Gospel of Christ: for it is the power of God unto salvation to every one that believeth; to the Jew first, and also to the Greek.

For therein is the righteousness of God revealed from faith to faith: as it is written, The just shall live by faith.''

Many times we have read these two verses and stopped at the end of verse 16. However, verse 17 tells us why the Gospel is the power of God. It is the power of God because "THEREIN IS THE RIGHTEOUSNESS OF GOD REVEALED ... "

A GOSPEL THAT DOES NOT REVEAL GOD'S RIGHTEOUSNESS HAS NO POWER.

The true Gospel of Jesus Christ is a revelation of how God has taken sinful man and made him a new creature and imparted unto him a perfect righteousness.

II Corinthians 5:21 tells us how God did this: "For He hath made Him (Jesus) to be sin for us, who knew no sin; that we might be made the righteousness of God in Him.''

Most Christians think that they are simply forgiven of their sins and that is all that happens in their salvation. That is only the beginning of what happens. God has done far more than forgive us our sins. He has imparted unto us His own nature and righteousness so that we can stand in His presence without shame or inferiority.

The Bible tells us, "Now the RIGHTEOUSNESS OF GOD without the law is manifested, being witnessed by the law and the prophets ... To declare, at this time His righteousness: That He might be just and the justifier of him which believeth in Jesus.'' (Romans 3:21 & 26)

A person who has been born again is a new creature in Christ Jesus. Listen to what God says about this new creature: "But of Him are ye in Christ Jesus, who of God is made unto us wisdom, and RIGHTEOUSNESS, and sanctification, and redemption.'' (I Corinthians 1:30)

4

God has said many things about the new man who lives on the inside of your body. You are born again. You need to believe what God says about you, and begin to see yourself as God sees you after you are born again.

JESUS DIED AND ROSE AGAIN TO MAKE YOU THE RIGHTEOUSNESS OF GOD.

II Corinthians 5:21 says, "For He hath made Him to be sin for us, who knew no sin; that we might be made the righteousness of God in Him."

The maker, the designer, of an automobile knows more about it than you do. The more you find out about it, the more you will appreciate it. God is your Maker and your Designer. He knows more about us than we know about ourselves. As you learn more and more about what He has done for you and how He has recreated you through the new birth, you will appreciate Him more and you will have power and victory in your life.

THE FRUIT OF RIGHTEOUSNESS

There is a fruit of righteousness. As a new creature, God says that you are to bring forth fruit (or evidence) of your new nature. Your new nature is a love nature with the righteousness of God. II Corinthians 9:10 tells us, "Now he that ministereth seed to the sower both minister bread for your food, and multiply your seed sown, and increase the FRUITS OF YOUR RIGHTEOUSNESS."

James 3:18 further states, "THE FRUIT OF RIGHTEOUSNESS is sown in peace of them that make peace."

According to Philippians 1:11, the new creature is to be ".. filled with the FRUITS OF RIGHTEOUSNESS, which are filled by Christ Jesus, unto the glory and praise of God."

5

When you know you are made righteous, the fruit of righteousness should show forth in your life. You should act righteous and lay hold of everything that is rightfully yours because of your right standing with God.

You are a new creature in Christ Jesus! You are not the kind of person you used to be. II Corinthians 5:17 reaffirms, "Therefore if any person is in Christ, the Messiah, he is a new creature altogether, a new creation, the old (previous moral and spiritual condition) has passed away. Behold the fresh and new has come!" (Amplified Version)

You need to realize your inheritance in Christ.

The greatest problem of man, especially the new creature, has been sin and sin-consciousness.

There has been a lack of "righteousness-consciousness" in the hearts and minds of God's people.

THE GREATEST NEED OF THE NEW CREATURE IS TO REALIZE HOW RIGHTEOUS HE IS IN CHRIST AND THEREFORE HOW BOLDLY HE CAN ACT AS A NEW CREATURE IN FACING SATAN AND DEMON FORCES!

When a man is conscious of his old sinful nature and is not conscious of his true righteous nature in Jesus Christ, he cannot stand confidently in the presence of God. Hebrews 4:16 says, "Let us therefore come boldly unto the throne of grace, that we may obtain mercy, and find grace to help in time of need." As new creatures we are entitled to come boldly to the throne of grace.

A sense of unworthiness, or a sense of condemnation paralyzes the new creature!

Every new creature needs to be free from this type of negativism and condemnation!

6

No matter how much God has done for you, until you realize that you are free from unrighteousness and you are made righteous in God, you will be paralyzed in your ability to minister to people in need.

AS LONG AS THERE IS A SENSE OF INFERIORITY, THERE CAN BE NO SENSE OF AUTHORITY!!!!

Just think of new creatures who are paralyzed, immobile, and not moving in the flow of God's blessings! The devil has tried to keep millions of Christians in fear and defeat by keeping them ignorant of the truth of their righteousness through Jesus Christ.

Some people say what we Christians need is more power. Others say we need more faith. Well, of course we need these, but what the new creature needs most of all is an understanding of the Word of God.

What you need as a new creature is to understand by the Holy Ghost what God has done for you in Christ.

You need to know you are righteous and without sin in the sight of God! You are totally without condemnation! Romans 8:1 says, "There is therefore now no condemnation to them which are in Christ Jesus, who walk not after the flesh, but after the Spirit."

When you understand this, faith will arise in your spirit just as naturally as breathing!

Power comes to you automatically because of the understanding you gain in knowing you are in right standing with God.

I would like to share with you a true story from my friend, Bill Lovick, who was for years a missionary to

7

Africa. This story is about a man by the name of Asomono. If anyone would be disqualified from being used of God, this man would be your number one choice. But, in this one incident of his life, you will see that God can take a man who felt like a weak worm of the dust, unworthy and incompetent, and yet through the revelation of the grace of God and the Blood of Jesus Christ, be changed into a mighty deliverer. I want you to read the story just as Bill Lovick told it in his own words:[1]

THE STORY OF ASOMONO

"I want to tell you a story about a boy, his name is Asomono. When he first came to the mission compound in Basari, he was naked. He said, "I want a job", he had a great big fetish around his neck, one around his waist and one around his ankle. He said, "I hear you are looking for a mason." I said, "Yes, are you a good mason?" He said, "Yes, I am a good mason." I thought, "Boy, this is my chance."

He was a hard worker. We made bricks together. Then I started him laying bricks. When I saw him begin to put those bricks on the wall, I thought, dear God, if this is a good mason don't show me a bad mason. He could lay a thousand bricks in the same wall and they would be a thousand different directions and a thousand different elevations and a thousand different poses. I said, "Boy, if you are a mason, meet me, I am president of the world."

He was a boy that loved God. He was saved and gave his heart to Christ. He burned his fetish and began to work in our church. He began to blossom and to come forth.

I would try to teach him, but he couldn't learn. Then one day he said, "Pastor, God wants me to go to Bible School." I scratched my head and I thought, "Dear God, if you told that boy to go to Bible School, you have made a mistake." I said, "You go and pray and I will pray and we will see." He went back and he prayed. He prayed and prayed and he prayed. He came four or five times and told me God wanted him to go to Bible School. I said, "You go back and pray."

I got a letter from Brother Arthur Wilson. He wrote and said, "Bill we need Bible School students desperately." I thought, Boy, if you knew the candidates that I had you would be desperate. So I told Asomono there was a chance for him. I packed him and his wife and two children in my pick-up truck. When I got up there I said, "Brother Wilson, I brought you a student." He said, "Bill, is he an intelligent student?" I said, "Brother Wilson, you wait and see. You'll probably get the surprise of your life." I went back to my station.

It was only about three weeks later I received a telegram. All it said was: "Come get your boy, Wilson." That was all. I drove up in the yard. I saw Brother Wilson, an old gray-headed man. I said, "Brother Wilson, what is wrong with you?" He said, "Lovick, we have had the high. We've had the low, we have had the dumb and we have had the extra dumb. But we have never had anyone as deep as this boy in ignorance." I said, "What is wrong with him?" He said, "For three weeks I have shown that boy the letter "A". I said, "Asomono, this is the letter that starts your name, a, a, a, a, a, now what is it?" He said that Asmono would take that paper. He would look at it head on, then he wold turn it side ways, then he would turn it up side down. Then he would say anything between "b" to "z". He never got the right letter. He said, "Bill take this boy. He can never learn on God's earth, he is too dumb to learn." I took Asomono. I said, "Asomono, tomorrow we are going back to Basari." Tears began to just pour down his face. He said, "You think I am a failure, Brother Wilson thinks I am a failure, the students think I am a failure. They say that I am so dumb that I can't even open a peanut shell and get the peanuts out of it. But Pastor, God is going to help me somewhere."

The next day I put him in the back of the truck. I watched him all the way to Basari. I saw the tears flowing down his cheeks. His head was bowed and he was calling upon God. We arrived at our station about midnight. He came around the front of the truck. He said, "Pastor just let us stay in the church tonight. We will find a place tomorrow." I took Asomono and I knelt down and I prayed, "Dear God, don't let this boy be too discouraged. Help him Lord somewhere to work for Thee." Asomono went into the church.

The next morning I went down to the church and he was in the church praying. He was calling out to God with all his heart and with all his soul. The next day I went down and again he was praying. He came and he said, "Pastor, can I go to the village of Kulunga. Can I not go there Pastor and work?" I had reserved that village for one of our young men who had a white shirt and a tie, and he could speak French like a Frenchman. I thought, "That is the man I want to go." Then I thought, "What can this boy do? He can't do any harm. Maybe I will let him go." Then I said, "No, Asomono, not yet. You just wait." The next morning I came down, there was Asomono in the prayer room once again with Bible opened to God. He was holding that Bible up in the face of God and he said, "Dear God, I can't read. I don't know what these pages mean; but dear God, every word I have heard your servant speak I have hidden those words in my heart. Oh God, let me preach the Word. Let me tell my people of your love, truth and power." That boy sought God with all of his heart. I went home and I felt like a heel. I said, "God, somehow help me not to miss your will. Help me not to look at the exterior but help me look at the heart of man." That boy and I had a prayer meeting that evening. I saw that boy as a soldier of Jesus Christ with a breastplate of God and with a shield and a sword. I saw him reap with a sword. I prayed, "Dear God, help me to help him."

He and I went out to this village. We built a little house. His wife and children moved out with him. Then together we built a little mud church. Asomono began to preach. He would come into the pastor's meeting and he would get up and say, "God is going to give us a work in Kulunga. God is going to give us souls in that city. Pray for us." Then I said, "Asomono, how many did you have in church Sunday?" "Four, myself, my wife, and my two little girls but God is going to help us, Pastor." I thought, "Boy, there is only one way and that is up. You can't go down any further than you are already."

One day I was home and two soldiers came to my door. They said, "Pastor, the Commandant wants you immediately in Kulunga. Your Pastor has gotten that whole

11

area in an uproar." I said, "What has he done?" They said, "We don't even know what he has done. We just have been sent to get you. The Commandant is there."

I drove up to Kulunga and I drove into the yard of that little church. There must have been twenty to thirty thousand people. They were around there for one hundred yards in every direction. They were screaming out, "Make him king! Make him king!" I thought, "My God, make him king. They are as crazy as he is." I went into the little house and I said,"What is wrong? Where is Asomono?" They said, "He is inside." I went in and there lying down on the floor with a grass mat under him and a grass mat on top of him was Asomono fast asleep. I thought, "Dear God, how can a man sleep with all this going on." I shook him and I said, "Asomono, what is wrong?" He said, "Pastor, nothing is wrong. God has met us. God has met us." He just began to shout and glorify God. I said, "Well, tell me and let me shout with you."

He said, "Pastor, do you know that man that used to run naked up and down the street of this village? Do you remember that man that jumped up on your jeep and stuck his head in the window? That man with the dirty filthy beard full of cow dung? That man that slobbered all over your car, do you remember?" I said, "Yes, I remember him." He said, "Pastor, just day before yesterday I was going through the market and I had been praying that God would do something that would shake this village for His glory and I saw that man. A voice said to me, 'You believe in healing. Lay your hands upon him.' I turned around and I wondered who was making fun of me. But I didn't see anybody. I went on and I bought some eggs. I thought I wouldn't even go back that way, but go back another way."

Let me interrupt Asonomo's story by saying this: You notice at this point he is filled with fear, inferiority and inability. He has no confidence. Without God's help he would have never been able to do anything. God had to help him know who he was in Jesus Christ. He had to get him to believe and act as though he was righteous. As long as he had a sense of inferiority, he could never act in bold authority. Within him had to come the sense and the knowledge of who he was in Christ. God had to get him to act like a son of God.

Now let me continue with Asomono's story:

"I went back the other way and there that man sat. God said to me, 'My Son, if you believe this day you shall see the glory of God'. He said, "Pastor, I didn't know what to do. I didn't want anybody to see me so I laid my eggs down real softly. I went over and I laid my hand on that man. I was going to pray real soft-like. But Pastor, you know that Spirit that comes on us when we are in the prayer room? That Spirit came on me right there in the middle of that market and I was lost and I began to pray and I began to shout to God with all of my might. When I opened my eyes everybody was there and this man stood up. He said, 'Take me home with you. Tell me about Jesus'." He said, "Pastor, I brought him home. I brought him a pair of my pants. My wife gave him some warm water to wash in and shave. That man sat down and asked me to tell him about Jesus. I told him about Jesus from beginning to end. Then he said, 'Tell it to me one more time.' Pastor, I told him again. I sat there all night long. After I finished, he said to my wife,'Tell it to me again'." He said for one night and one day we have done nothing but sit and tell that man about Christ. Pastor, yesterday that man opened up his heart and Jesus came into his heart and washed his sins away.

I said, "But, Asomono, that doesn't answer my question. Why are all of these people here?" He said, "Pastor, do you know this man?" I said, "No." He said, "That man is Yandi. 'Yandi' in the Basari means the King, the High King. This man was to have been chief over two million people that spread into Ghana, into Togo and into Dohomey. But this man's brother poisoned him. This man has a Bachelor of Science degree from the University of Paris. When he came back at the death of his father, his brother poisoned him and he became the maniac that ran in the market eating the garbage and throwing dung on his body, an insane man." I said, "Where is he now?" He said, "He is with the elders."

"The Elders of the Basari Nation have heard of it and they have come and asked him to dethrone his brother and become King. There will be a political war." There would have been a war like that country had never seen. The Commandant had come and had asked to see me. I went to see him and he said, "Pastor, please try to do something. If this man wants his place there will be bloodshed. The nation is almost divided straight down the middle. Pastor, do what you can."

I went to see Yandi and talk to him. There he sat in robes of a Basari King with the Elders sitting around him. When he saw me he came to the door. He said, "Oh, you are Pastor Lovick," I said "Yes." He said,

"You are the man who sent Asomono." I hung my head and I said, "No, I am not the man that sent Asomono. It was God who sent him." I asked, "Yandi, what do you want to do? Do you want to be king?" He said, "Pastor, I can do nothing without asking my friend what to do." He said, "Would you leave me for a moment and I will see?" He sent me out. He sent the Elders out. He sent everybody out. I was wondering who he was going to call. I waited five minutes. I waited eight minutes, ten minutes. Then I looked through that little bamboo door. Where do you think he was? He was down on his knees praying to God. When he got through he came out. He said, "Pastor, I have the answer. No, I don't want to be King. I want to be something greater than King, I want to be a preacher like Asomono. I want to tell my people about Christ, about the Saviour of the world. If Asomono will tell me about God, and show me how to preach, I will teach him how to read and I will teach him how to write."

Friends, you may be ignorant, but in the hands of God, you can believe and you can be an answer in the cause of Almighty God to work and labour, even as Asomono. Today, Asomono is one of the greatest African evangelists that Africa has every known! "For it is not by might, nor by power, but it is by the Spirit of Almighty God." (Zechariah 4:6)

This is what we need in the body of Christ! We don't need fearful, whining, complaining, ineffective people of God. We need those who will rise up with a sense of authority and righteousness and act the part of a child of God. With this, we will bring miracles and deliverance to our generation. But, we will never do it until we realize and then begin to act like we are righteous. It is our responsibility to act like the sons and daughters of God. We need a sense of righteousness and this will come as we learn to renew our minds.

REPROGRAMMING YOUR MIND

As long as the devil can keep your mind ignorant of the truth about your righteousness as revealed in the Word of God, you will live under the dark cloud of unworthiness and condemnation. That is living under the devil's lie!

Romans 12 verses 1 and 2 tell us: "I beseech you therefore, brethren, by the mercies of God, that ye present your bodies a living sacrifice, holy, acceptable unto God, which is your reasonable service. And be not conformed to this world: but be ye transformed by the renewing of your mind, that ye may prove what is that good, and acceptable, and perfect will of God."

The spirit-man is made a new creation. You are a spirit being. You live in a body. When you are born again, you obtain absolute righteousness and perfect standing with God as a new creature.

However, your mind is like a computer. God did not give you a new mind instantaneously when you were born again. As the natural man, you lived according to your mind. (Ephesians 2:3) For many years you have listened to your mind and as a computer it reacts and believes certain things. Even though you are a new creature in your spirit, you need to have your computer (your mind) renewed or reprogrammed. Without God it is programmed according to the dictates of the flesh and the course of this world. It is programmed to follow after your old sinful nature.

Ephesians 2:2 tells us that before your spirit was born again, you walked "according to the course of this world, according to the prince of the power of the air, the spirit that now worketh in the children of disobedience."

Ephesians 2:3 continues, "Among whom also we all had our conversation (manner of life) in times past in the lusts of our flesh, fulfilling the desires of the flesh and of the mind; and were by nature the children of wrath, even as others."

Some people have had their minds programmed with religious traditions contrary to the Word of God. They must reprogram their thinking to be in harmony with the Bible. Religion has taught God's new creature to say, "I am not worthy." But the Word of God says of the new creature, "There is therefore NOW NO CONDEMNATION to those who are in Christ Jesus." (Romans 8:1)

The devil whispers, "You are going to die of sickness." But when you have reprogrammed your mind with God's Word, you will quickly say, "I will not die. God will satisfy me with long life. (Ps. 91:16) I will not have sickness, for Jesus says that 'By His stripes I am healed'." (Isaiah 53:5)

The devil whispers, "You are going under. You will never make it financially." But the new creature whose mind is reprogrammed boldly says, "My God will supply all my need according to His riches in glory by Christ Jesus." (Philippians 4:19) The devil whispers, "You are a sinner and you have failed God.

17

You are not worthy." But you boldly say what God says about you, "I am the righteousness of God." Declare John 3:17 is true: "For God sent not his son into the world to condemn the world; but that the world through him might be saved."

The new creature must constantly be reprogramming his computerlike mind. Daily you must feed your mind upon the Word of God. This process will never end!

You need your mind renewed by understanding the Bible and knowing who you are in Christ, your abilities in Him and your standing through the Blood of Jesus.

Your mind must be taught to think like the Bible speaks. You have no right as a new creature to take any other attitude than what God says about your situation.

Let me tell you a story which illustrates this great need for developing your mind. One time I drove past a man who was standing in front of a large, expensive home. As I looked at that strong, muscular, handsome-looking man from a distance, I had several thoughts.

He appeared to be a man that had distinguished himself in athletics. He could well have been lauded by many as a great athlete. However, He was not.

He could have been a great musician with those fine hands playing many instruments. He could have possibly even been a scientist. He could have been one of those unique contributors to the needs of humanity. He could have been a medical doctor. He could well have been an executive in some corporation. He could have had hundreds of employees under him and a multi-million dollar bank account.

Oh, what he could have been!

Yet, when I got close to him and I beheld that strong, healthy body, with all of it's potentiality, he talked with the intellect of a young boy, possibly nine or ten years old.

His mind had ceased to be developed!

What a loss!

Who knows what he could have done for the Lord and the human race!

Do you see what a tragedy it is when the natural mind ceases to develop?

Think of this same principle in the spiritual realm. There are men and women that we meet in the Body of Christ who could have taken continents for God. They could have done mighty exploits for the Lord. The could have blessed millions of needy people! They could have walked with God and prospered so as to give millions of dollars to the kingdom of God and the Gospel!

But they never did.

They have prattled on with undeveloped minds, unrenewed by the Word of God, living like little babies crying and fussing over every little thing. They are living on a "bottle" when they should be doing mighty miracles for God!

As long as the devil can keep your mind ignorant and dwarfed, he can keep you living under the dark cloud of unworthiness, defeat and condemnation. You need to have your mind renewed by an understanding of the Bible. You need to know who you are, your abilities in God and your standing through the Blood of the Lord Jesus Christ. Every day you must develop and renew your mind. Every day you must let God's thoughts go into your mind. You must meditate upon God's Word.

Many Christians could be living victorious, powerful, useful lives; but instead they are weak, defeated, fearful, and living under condemnation. It is because their minds have never been renewed to know who they really are as new creatures in Christ.

As a new creature, you especially need to renew your mind on the subject of the righteousness of God. You need to know, think, talk, and act like you are righteous and free from condemnation in God's sight! (And you are!)

The Bible says in II Corinthians 5:17 & 21, "Therefore if any man be in Christ, he is a new creature: old things are passed away; behold, all things are become new. For He hath made Him to be sin for us, who knew no sin; that we might be made the RIGHTEOUSNESS OF GOD IN HIM."

A RIGHTEOUSNESS LIFE-STYLE

You are a new creation. You are to be an example of the righteousness of God on this earth.

Romans 5:17 tells us, "For if by one man's offence death reigned by one; much more they which receive abundance of grace and of the GIFT OF RIGHTEOUSNESS SHALL REIGN IN LIFE by one, Jesus Christ."

God wants you to reign in righteousness IN THIS LIFE! God wants you to be an example of His righteousness right here on earth. Philippians 2:15 & 16 further explains how we are to be blameless in the midst of a "crooked and perverse nation." Certainly that describes the condition of our day! Of course there will not be a "crooked and perverse nation" in heaven, so naturally you can see that God wants you to show His righteousness NOW.

There is a natural reaction in a person who knows he is righteous. KNOWING YOU HAVE NO CONDEMNATION AND KNOWING THAT YOU ARE RIGHTEOUS IN THE SIGHT OF GOD CAUSES YOU TO LIVE AND ACT LIKE JESUS DID IN THE FACE OF LIFE, DEATH, DEMONS, DISEASE AND CIRCUMSTANCES!

I know of no better illustration of living a life of righteousness than this story of my friend, Terry Mize, who is actively doing missionary work all over the world. I will simply let him share in his own words, the experience that he had in Old Mexico:[2]

"On my way to Guadalajara, and as I pulled out of Zacatecas, I saw a hitch-hiker standing by the side of the road. At first, I passed him by, but then I was really impressed that the man needed Jesus. Now, God didn't speak to me and tell me to pick him up, or anything like that. I just stopped the car, backed up, and picked him up, and we started off down the road. As I was gathering my Spanish together to tell him about Jesus, I turned to say something to him, and there he sat with a gun in his hand. When he saw me look at the gun, he shoved it into my ribs, reached up with his left hand and grabbed my collar, as he started screaming and yelling at the me: "I'm going to kill you!"

I said, "You can't do that. I am a man of God." Again he screamed and yelled at me that he was going to kill me. And again, I said, "You can't do that, I am a man of God."

The first thing that happened, when I saw the gun in his hand, was my heart jumped up in my throat. It scared me! But I know enough about the Word of God to know that fear and faith are opposites. Fear is the opposite force of faith. Satan is motivated by fear and God is motivated by faith. Faith and fear cannot operate in the same place. I knew that. So — I got rid of that fear. It wasn't any big deal. I simply said, "God has not given me the spirit of fear, but of love, and of power, and of a sound mind. Fear has torment, but perfect love casteth out fear. God is love, and I have God. So fear, get out of here in the Name of Jesus. I am not tolerating you."

After I had dispatched fear, I had to deal with another situation, mental assent. I believe that it was Frances Hunter who called people, "Goat Christians." They say, "I believe the Word of God — but." They are always "butting" everything. "Sure, I believe the Word of God says that we are healed by the stripes of Jesus — but, I have this pain." And, "I know that, but the bank book is empty." That is mentally assenting to the Word of God. You start believing it — but. You are inclined to go with the circumstances.

Anyway, I had to know that I know that I know that I believe the Word of God. I had a tape going in the tape player, by Kenneth Copeland, titled the integrity of the Word of God. I just let it keep on playing. I figured that if there was a time that I needed to hear that, it was certainly a good time! As I kept driving, the hitch-hiker kept screaming at me, that he was going to kill me, and I kept on saying, "You can't do that. I am a man of God. I have authority over you in the Name of Jesus. You can't kill me; you can't harm me in any way.''

He couldn't understand that. According to the world's system, it didn't look as though I had authority over the situation.

If you had been sitting out there beside the road in a bleacher, watching all of that taking place whom would you have thought was winning? Most people would have said, ''The guy with the gun.'' That is according to the world's system. But the Bible says, ''The man with the Word of God wins!''

I rebuked that hitch-hiker in English; I rebuked him in Spanish, and I rebuked him in tongues. I reminded God what His Word said. I told the devil what the Word of God had to say, and I told the man what the Word of God had to say. I was hearing it all. I was reminding myself of the Word of God. In fact my mind was going a million miles a minute. You know how your mind functions when there is an emergency. The devil brought back to me everything that I had seen on TV. I thought about slamming on the brakes and grabbing the gun . . . I thought about it all! My friend, Jerry Savelle was telling abut this one time, and he said, ''If Terry's mind had been renewed to Starsky and Hutch, or Barretta, he would have tried to do what they had done, but since his mind was renewed to the Word of God, he used the Word of God.''

You have to keep your Word level higher than any other level. I was glad that I knew that the Word of God was life to me. I was in a situation where I had an opportunity to NOT live very long.

I told that hitch-hiker that I was a minister. He didn't know what a minister was. I told him I was a preacher, he knew nothing about a preacher. I told him I was like a priest, and being that Mexico was mostly Catholic, he knew what a priest was. But he wasn't in too good of a standing with his local church, and he wasn't very impressed that I was a priest.

He just kept telling me that he was going to kill me, and I kept telling him that he wasn't going to kill me.

I said to God, "Now God, the Word of God says that Jesus said that I have authority or power over all authority of the enemy. ALL! And nothing, NOTHING shall by any means hurt me." This is why I released my faith with my words, which I was glad about later on. I said, "God, if he pulls the trigger, my job is to believe Your Word, and Your job is to do something about that bullet." I know that may sound funny now, but it was not funny then. I said, "Your job is to do something with that bullet and you don't have much room to work with seeing that the barrel is against my side." I said that to God because I believed it, and I still believe it today.

I have shared this testimony, and some people have come up to me and said, "I have a testimony just like that, except I got robbed." I tell them that their testimony is not really exactly like mine. If I start checking on them I find out where they have missed it. One man told me that he had a testimony just like mine, except he got shot. He said, "I picked up a hitch-hiker who pulled a gun on me, and I said 'Hallelujah!' and he shot me."

I said, "Well, it was what you said." The difference is in what you say.

It is like a lady who wrote me a letter one time from South Mexico. She wrote, "Terry, I wish that you had been here with your faith and deliverance ministry, but you probably couldn't have handled this guy either. He was

24

demon-possessed. We had him locked up, but he broke loose and he came after my husband. My husband said, "The blood of Jesus has power.' The guy hit him anyway."

I told the lady that her husband might just as well said, "The grass is green and the sky is blue." All he did was make a statement of truth. Sure, the Blood of Jesus has power, but he could have said, "The sun is going to rise tomorrow," and he would have made a statement of truth. The man should have said, "Satan! Stop right there! You'll not touch God's anointed! Don't you take another step! Now you get out of him in the Name of Jesus!" The difference is in what you say.

I kept saying this to the hitch-hiker, and he kept getting madder and madder at me. Every time the devil kept bringing thoughts to my mind, I would just reach up and catch myself by the ear with my left hand and I would say, "Now Terry, you say what the Word of God says. You handle this in the spirit."

You know, Elijah just said, "Let us let God be God. If Baal is god then we will serve him, and if God is God, we will serve Him." And God showed Himself strong, and Elijah killed all the prophets of Baal.

I said, "God, I am going to let you be God. I am going to handle this in the spirit. I refuse to do anything in the flesh. I'm going to use the Word of God on this guy, and I am going to have to win. I am more than a conqueror!"

Well, the more I talked the madder he got; it didn't make any sense to him. He had the gun in my ribs, the hammer cocked, and his finger on the trigger. Once, he asked me, "Aren't you afraid?"

I said, "Why should I be afraid? All you've got is a loaded gun and I've got the Name of Jesus." He reached

25

down and picked up one of the microphens that I had lying on the seat beside me. I said, "Put that down. I belongs to God. Everything in this car belongs to God. I belong to God: the car belongs to God, and you can't have any of it."

That just made him madder, and he said, "Pull off over in this cornfield, off on the side of the road. Pull in there!" I pulled into the cornfield, and he reached over and grabbed the keys out of the ignitions, and yelled, "Get out!" I got out of the car on my side, and he got out on his side, and he ordered me to go to the front of the car. "Give my your money, your watch, your rings, and sunglasses ...," you know, everything he could see. "Lay it on the ground there, and then back up." I did as I was told, and he walked up, bent down, and picked it all up.

When he got close to me, I stuck my finger in his face and said, "I rebuke you in the Name of Jesus Christ of Nazareth."

He stuck his gun between my eyes; hammer still cocked; finger on the trigger, and he was wildly slinging his left hand, "Shut up! If you say one more word, I'll kill you!" he yelled.

I stuck my finger back up in his face, past his gun, and said, "I rebuke you in the Name of Jesus Christ of Nazareth, and you cannot kill or hurt me in any way!" Instantly that hitch-hiker jumped back, lowered his gun, and shot at me five times. I counted them! I honestly, do not know where the gun was pointed, but I do remember what I said, and what happened. I assumed that he was aiming at me, since he had said that if I said another word he was going to kill me. I stood there, leaning up against my car, and all five of those bullets were hitting between my feet. I didn't move. The hitch-hiker looked kind of puzzled. He backed off, reloaded his gun, and as he came nearer to me, he said, "Start walking."

I walked out into the cornfield, saying, "Greater is He that is in me, than he that is in the world ... The Word of God works ... I have authority over the enemy ...!"

After we had walked about 150 yards or so, he said, "Take your clothes off!" And I stood there — God's man of faith and power — in a cornfield in Mexico, in my underwear. But I was still winning! When he saw that he could not kill me, he decided to rob me. He took my clothes, and with my car keys in his hand, he turned around and walked off: fully intending to get into my car and drive off. I said, "God, I have done what Your Word says to do. I have not operated in the flesh. I have taken authority. I have done everthing. Either Your Word works or it doesn't. I believe that it works. If it doesn't, I'm not going to pay any attention to it any more. I'll throw it away. But I believe that it works. It has kept me from being killed, but he can't rob me either. And he has full intention of getting into my car ... " When he was about 20 yards from my car, I said, "God, this is not one of those times when I need an answer day after tomorrow. I need an answer right now!" I yelled at the man, "I charge you in the Name of Jesus to come back here!"

The man didn't break his stride as he made a 180 degree turn, and came back to where I was standing. He threw my clothes at me and said, "Put them on!" As I put my clothes back on, he asked, "What is it

27

that you want to talk to me about?" He acted as though I had made an appointment with him.

"I don't want to talk to you about anything else. I am telling you that I am a man of God. you have found out that you cannot rob or kill me. I am going home.

They have a saying in Mexico: "Mi casa es su casa:" which means, "My house is your house." I said, "If you want to go home with me, I'll help you in any way possible. But we aren't playing your game any more."

He shook his head and said, "You know, I like you!" He put his gun in his belt as he said, "I'm going to put my confidence in you." When we got to the car, he took his gun out again, and said, "I'm going to drive. You sit in the back."

"No!" I told him. "I'm a man of God. I have authority over you: You can't do anything, and I have all the authority in the Name of Jesus. It is my car, and I am going to drive. You can go or stay here. Now, give me my keys in Jesus' Name." The man handed me my keys, we got into my car and drove off. I told him that Jesus came and died for him, was resurrected for him, and is sitting on the right hand of the Father making intercession for him.

We came to a little place called "Jalpa"; about half-way between Zacatecas and Guadalajara. He said, "I cannot go to Guadalajara with you. Take me up into the mountains, I have some friends up in the Sierras."

I consented to do this. He showed me where to turn off, and we made our turn, right into three policemen, leaning against a police car in front of the police station. He pulled his gun out and said, "Don't you do anything, or I will kill you first, and as many policemen as I can before they kill me."

I said, "What do I need them for? I've got the Name of Jesus."

"Oh yeah!" he said, as he put his gun back up and we drove on up into the mountains for about thirty miles.

Finally I stopped and said, "Look, I can't take you any farther. I just have enough gas to get to Guadalajara, and I have given you all of my money ($2.00). I would give you more if I had it: I only have enough gas to get home, so — I am going home. You can either get out, or you can go home with me."

"I'll get out." he said.

I gave him some food and things that I had brought back from Houston, and he reached into his pockets and pulled out my watch, rings, and all the things that he had taken from me. "You can have that," I said. He said "You're giving it to me?" I said, "You can't take it from me, you can't rob me. Just give me my wedding ring, and you can have my other rings, my watch, and all the other stuff." I said, "Now, I'll pray for you before you get going." I laid my hands on the hitch-hiker and prayed for him, and told him where he could find me in Guadalajara, if he wanted to find me. He walked up into the mountains as I drove toward Guadalajara and my family.

That night, I am sure that the man sat up there in the mountains, looked at his gun, and wondered why he wasn't a rich man. The equipment that I had with me cost thousands of dollars in the States, and three times that price in Mexico. He could have been a wealthy man.

The gun is supposed to represent power and authority, according to the world's system. But the authority of God's Word is where it is! The Word of God works.

You see, Terry Mize could act the way he did because he knew that he was righteous and therefore he had authority. Without this knowledge of righteousness, he would have had a sense of inferiority and the results of this encounter would have been vastly different. Thank God we can boldly say, "I AM THE RIGHTEOUSNESS OF GOD IN CHRIST!!"

There is a fruit of righteousness and it expresses itself in your life as you obey God. You are to be filled "with the fruits of righteousness."

When a person really knows that he is righteous, when he knows it deep in his heart and it is sure in his understanding; then when the devil tempts him or talks to him, he does not believe the devil's lies. HE KNOWS HE IS RIGHTEOUS!

There are certain actions that he will have and there are certain fruits he will produce. His life will reflect his righteous standing in God. New creatures who come to realize how righteous they are produce fruits that other Christians without this knowledge do not produce.

When you live under condemnation, you do not move in faith.

When you realize that you are righteous, you produce the fruit of righteousness. Paul the Apostle said that you are to be filled with these fruits of righteousness. God has made and declared you legally righteous in His sight!

Right now, boldly declare out loud:

I know that I have no condemnation in the sight of God! I know it because the Bible says, "There is therefore now no condemnation to them which are in Christ Jesus, who walk not after the flesh, but after the Spirit." (Romans 8:1)

I know I am made righteous in the sight of God! I know it because the Bible says, "Therefore if any man be in Christ, he is a new creature; old things are passed away; behold, all things are become new." (II Corinthians 5:17)

I know I have boldness to enter into God's presence by the Blood of Jesus. I know it because the Bible says, "Let us therefore come boldly unto the throne of grace, that we may obtain mercy, and find grace to help in time of need." (Hebrews 4:16)

I know that God looks upon me as if I had never sinned! I know it because the Bible says, "If we confess our sins, he is faithful and just to forgive us our sins, and to cleanse us from all unrighteousness." (I John 1:9)

This causes me to live and act like Jesus!

I have victory in the face of life, death, demons, the devil, disease and circumstances.

I know, as a new creature, my inner man is just as righteous as Jesus!

THE LIFE OF THE SPIRIT MAN

Does the new creature have spiritual death or eternal life?

There is no spiritual death whatsoever in the new creature! God said, "For God so loved the world, that He gave His only begotten Son, that whosoever believeth in Him should not perish, but have everlasting life." (John 3:16)

God said that He has made us to be the "RIGHTEOUSNESS OF GOD IN CHRIST." (II Corinthians 5:21)

Because you are just as righteous as God, you need not be concerned with failing or the fear of failure. Every one of us falls short once in a while, but the Blood of Jesus Christ cleanses us from all unrighteousness.

I John 1:7 & 9 says, "If we walk in the light, as He is in the light, we have fellowship one with another, and the Blood of Jesus Christ His Son cleanseth us from all sin. If we confess our sins, He is faithful and just to forgive us our sins, and to cleanse us from all unrighteousness."

You are not saved by your actions or your works. Ephesians 2:8 & 9 says, "For by grace are ye saved through faith; and that not of yourselves; it is the gift of God: Not of works, lest any man should boast."

There is a new man, a spirit man, living on the inside of you and he is righteous! He is in right standing with God through Jesus Christ. God says it is so! God cannot lie!

When a Christian makes a mistake and sins, he feels grieved. Why?

He feels grieved because he has been made righteous and that righteous nature within him abhors sin.

Many new creatures have tried to go back into the world and sin again after being reborn, but they cannot do it with peace and joy. Their hearts break. Sin grieves the God-man within them. They cannot live like they used to. They are new creatures. Their place is in God!

JESUS - OUR EXAMPLE

Look at Jesus. He had no spiritual death in His spirit. He was the first man since Adam that ever stood on this earth and had no spiritual death in His spirit. Adam had no spiritual death in the beginning, but he received spiritual death (the nature of satan) after he sinned. Jesus came as the Last Adam.

He was the first man since Adam and Eve to stand on the face of the earth without a sense of sin.

He had no unrighteousness in Him.

The prince of this world came to Him and He was able to say, "You have nothing in Me." I like what Jesus said regarding satan (Amplified Bible): "He has no claim on Me!

He has nothing in common with Me!

There is nothing in Me that belongs to him!

He has no power over Me!" (John 14:30)

Therefore since Jesus was a man of righteousness and He had no spiritual death, there should be the fruit of righteousness in his life. These are some of the fruits of righteousness:

Jesus had no fear of the Father!

Oh, how He loved the Father! He did not say, "God is trying to kill me with sickness and disease. God put evil on me to teach me something. I am afraid God is mad at me."

NO!

There was no fear because He knew the love of the Father.

There was no fear of demons!

He stood before satan himslef and said, "It is written." (Luke 4) He defeated satan with God's Word. He was worthy to speak as God speaks because He was the righteousness of God — just as you are.

He said to demons, "Be gone! I charge you to come out of him." Instantly, demons obeyed Jesus. Six-thousand demons left a man instantly at the simple command of this man Jesus who ahs the assurance of righteousness. (Mark 5)

This is the way a man lives and conducts his life who is righteous.

This is the way a man lives who knows he has no spiritual death. This is the way a man lives who knows he has direct access to the Father.

There is no fear of man, demons or disease. "The law of the Spirit of life in Christ Jesus has made you free from the law of sin and death." (Romans 8:2)

Jesus lived unafraid of the Father, unafraid of the devil, unafraid of men's opinions, unafraid of sickness, disease, demons or circumstances.

Jesus is the example of what every new creature should be.

He was a man who knew His ability and power in God. He stood before the people in synagogues and said, "The Spirit of the Lord is upon Me, because He hath anointed Me to preach the Gospel to the poor; He hath sent Me to heal the brokenhearted, to preach deliverance to the captives, and recovering of sight to the blind, to set at liberty them that are bruised, to preach the acceptable year of the Lord." (Luke 4:18 & 19)

He told people at He came to announce to the

human race that NOW is the time for God to do this for them!

That is the way a new creature acts when he knows he is righteous. Jesus was the first-born new creature. He is the first-born among MANY brethren. (Romans 8:29)

YOU MUST BELIEVE GOD'S WORD

God has said that you are the righteousness of God in Christ. Righteous means being in right standing with God. When you are born again you are automatically put in right standing as a son with his Heavenly Father. You are not to rely on your feelings nor on your circumstances for this assurance.

You must believe God's Word!

In Matthew 14:29, Peter got out of the boat and walked on the water. He was doing real well until he started to look at the storm. As long as he looked at Jesus — JESUS, THE WORD OF GOD — he could walk on the water.

When you start looking at your circumstances of your past life, the devil will bring you under condemnation and you may begin to sink. KEEP LOOKING AT THE WORD OF GOD! You will walk supernaturally. Keep your eyes on God's Word. Keep your eyes on the written Word — the Bible, and the Living Word — Jesus.

Many times the devil told me that I would die. I would not listen to him. Instead, I looked at the Word of God and kept "walking on the water". The devil could not make me sink. The Word of God upheld me.

Hebrews 1:3 says that "God upholds all things by

the Word of His power.''

His Word was what I was walking on. I kept confessing these scriptures, ''The number of thy days I will fulfill.'' (Exodus 23:26)

''By His stripes I am healed.'' (Isaiah 53:5)

''Christ hath redeemed me from the curse of the law.'' (Galatians 3:13) The curse of the law includes every sickness and every disease. Therefore, I will not take sickness or disease from the devil.

Jesus is the Surety of the New Covenant. He stands behind every Word in the New Testament.

He became sin that we might become the righteousness of God! (II Corinthians 5:21)

The Bible says that new creatures are ''created in righteousness and true holiness!'' (Ephesians 4:24)

Because Jesus is the FIRST-born among MANY brethren, we know that God wants many others to enter into the family of God because they will receive a righteous nature and they will live and act like Jesus. That is God's plan.

YOU ARE GOD'S WORKMANSHIP

In talking about the new creature, Paul says this: ''And you hath He quickened (made alive), who were dead in trespasses and sins.

Wherein in time past ye walked according to the course of this world, according to the prince of the power of the air, the spirit that now worketh in the children of disobedience:

Among whom also we all had our conversation in times past in the lusts of our flesh fulfilling the desires of the flesh and of the mind: and were by nature the children of wrath, even as others.

But God, who is rich in mercy, for His great love wherewith He loved us,

Even when we were dead in sins, hath quickened us (made alive) together with Christ, (by grace ye are saved;)

And hath raised us up together, and made us sit together in heavenly places in Christ Jesus:

That in the ages to come He might show the exceeding riches of His grace in His kindness toward us through Christ Jesus.

For by grace are ye saved through faith; and that not of yourselves: it is the gift of God:

Not of works, lest any man should boast.

For we are His workmanship, created in Christ Jesus unto good works, which God hath before ordained that we should walk in them.'' (Ephesians 2:1-10)

YOU ARE GOD'S WORKMANSHIP!

The new creature inside of you is God's masterpiece. You are created in Christ Jesus unto good works.

Romans 8:29 says, "For whom He did foreknow, He also did predestinate to be conformed to the image of His Son, that He might be the firstborn among many brethren."

Many people think that being a new creature refers to what we will be in heaven. They believe it refers to us as living in resurrected bodies. That is not so! When you *live* in the Word, *walk* in the Word, live *by* the Word, let *your mind be renewed* by the Word, and *believe* the Word, YOU LOOK JUST LIKE JESUS TO THE DEVIL! You look just like Jesus to every demon.

ACTING RIGHTEOUS

When you walk towards the devil and demon powers, they tremble. Why?

You have the righteousness of Jesus Christ! You have His life! You have His Blood! You have His Spirit! You have His Word! You have His love! You look just like Jesus. No wonder the devil trembles!

This is why the Bible tells you to "resist the devil and he will flee from you." (James 4:7)

When you act like God told you the truth, you look just like Jesus. The thing you need to do is to start acting like Him more and more.

Let there be no fear of the Father!

Let there be no fear of satan and demons!

Let there be no fear of man!

Let there be no fear of disease!

Let there be no fear of circumstances!

Know the ability and power available to you in Christ and begin to act like God told you the truth.

THIS IS THE LIFE OF RIGHTEOUSNESS!

This is a result of knowing that you are in right standing with God!

THIS IS THE NEW CREATURE'S NUMBER ONE NEED!

With a mind renewed by the Word of God, you can resist the devil and demons and they will flee.

You can stay free from sickness and disease and live in divine health.

You will say, "I can do all things through Christ who strengtheneth me." (Philippians 4:13)

You will say, "Greater is He that is in me than he that is in the world." (I John 4:4)

You will agree with Jesus who said to us, "In My Name you shall cast out devils; you shall speak with new tongues; you shall take up serpents; and if you drink any deadly thing, it will not hurt you; you shall lay hands on the sick and they shall recover." (Mark 16:17-18)

This is what the Bible means when it talks about being filled with the fruits of righteousness. When you know you are righteous, you will give expression to that new nature inside of you and it will bring forth fruit for the kingdom of God.

There is no condemnation for the new creature. There is no sense of sin, guilt, sickness or disease. Tell your mind what God says about you in His Word. Let the Word sink into your spirit.

Realize that you are made righteous through faith. Philippians 3:9 says, "And be found in Him, not having my own righteousness which is of the law, but that which is through the faith of Christ, the righteousness which is of God by faith."

This righteousness is a gift of God!

You cannot earn it!

It is a gift!

It is your position in the kingdom of God imparted unto you in salvation. You are made righteous by God through Jesus Christ. As surely as Jesus took your sin, He gave you His righteousness!

Romans 8:31-39 says, "What shall we then say to these things? If God be for us, who can be against us?

He that spared not His own Son, but delivered Him up for us all, how shall He not with Him also freely give us all things?

Who shall lay any thing to the charge of God's elect? It is God that justifieth.

Who is he that condemneth? It is Christ that died, yea rather, that is risen again, who is even at the right hand of God, who also maketh intercession for us.

Who shall separate us from the love of Christ? Shall tribulation, or distress, or persecution, or famine, or nakedness, or peril, or sword?

As it is written, For thy sake we are killed all the day long; we are accounted as sheep for the slaughter.

Nay, in all these things we are more than conquerors through Him that loved us.

For I am persuaded, that neither death, nor life, nor angels, nor principalities, nor powers, nor things present, nor things to come.

Nor height, nor depth, nor any other creature, shall be able to separate us from the love of God, which is in Christ Jesus our Lord.''

YOU ARE CREATED IN THE IMAGE OF JESUS. You are conformed to the image of God. You are God's elect. Who shall lay anything to your charge!!!

Do you think that a Man who died for you, bore your sins, went to hell for you, conquered the devil for you, ascended to the Father and took His Blood to heaven, sat down at the right hand of God and lives to intercede for you will condemn you?

NO! NO! NO! HE WILL NOT CONDEMN YOU!!

Do you remember when Jesus — that first-born new creature who had no spiritual death nor condemnation in Him and who was perfectly righteous, was approached by demons? They said, "Oh, are you going to torment us before our time?"

That is the picture of the attitude of demosn in the spirit world when a new creature without condemnation, without spiritual death, and perfectly righteous in the sight of God comes on the scene. Philippians 2:10-11 says, "That at the Name of Jesus every knee should bow, of things in heaven, and things in earth, and things under the earth. And that every tongue should confess that Jesus Christ is Lord, to the glory of God the Father."

Always picture the devil as weak, defeated, dethroned and shaking in fear. He trembles when he hears the sound of the footsteps of a new creature coming!

Always picture satan afraid of you, and running from you. He is a shattered, torn, defeated, conquered foe. That defeated devil is no match for the new creature! "And having spoiled principalities and powers, he made a shew of them openly, triumphing over them in it (the cross.)" Colossians 2:15

Satan is under your feet. It is good to look downward when speaking to him. He is under you! He is below you!

If your mind has not been renewed by the Word, the devil will try to make you think that he is a giant. The Bible says, "He goeth about AS a roaring lion." (I Peter 5:8) He acts AS a lion. He is trying to imitate Jesus, who is the True Lion of the Tribe of Judah! That true Lion lives in you!!!

Picture yourself as a conqueror. Picture yourself like Jesus. Picture the spirit world reacting to you just like it reacted to Jesus.

Let me say this: Learning all you are as a new creature will not come instantly. You will need to practice, believe and renew your mind continually in the Word of God. Do not contradict what God says about you in His Word by what you say with your mouth! Correct yourself if you do. Talk, believe and act like you are righteous.

If you do something wrong and you are grieved in your spirit, say, "Thank you, Father, that I am righteous. I cannot agree with what I did. Forgive me." (I John 1:9)

Instantly the sin is forgiven because the inner man is so righteous that he cannot stand to have sin practiced in his life and conduct.

This is how the righteousness of God works in your life. You have God's Word as your assurance that you are the righteousness of God in Christ. No matter what the devil tries to do to you, you have already been made righteous. You are a new creature in Christ Jesus. Something happened when you sincerely took Jesus into your heart. If the powers of darkness try to attach themselves to you and beat you down, you can say this:

I AM MORE THAN A CONQUEROR IN JESUS' NAME! (Romans 8:37)

I AM RECREATED IN CHRIST JESUS! (II Corinthians 5:17)

I AM THE RIGHTEOUSNESS OF GOD IN CHRIST! (II Corinthians 5:21)

I BELONG TO GOD AND I AM HIS WORKMANSHIP! (Ephesians 2:10)

THE BLOOD OF JESUS HAS CLEANSED ME FROM ALL UNRIGHTEOUSNESS! (I John 1:9)

42

I STAND BEFORE THE FATHER, THE ANGELS AND DEMONS AND BOLDLY DECLARE THAT I AM WORTHY TO RECEIVE ALL OF THE BLESSINGS AND PROMISES OF GOD! (Hebrews 4:16)

You are now ready to cast off the garments of guilt, sin and condemnation.

DO IT NOW!

In Jesus' Name hurl these things back into the face of satan!

NOW STAND TALL FOR JESUS! YOU ARE RIGHTEOUS!

March forth into the arena of human need and win the lost, deliver the captives and bring healing to the sick.

You will enjoy abundant life as you *practice the truth* you have learned in this book.

[1]WHO OR WHAT IS JESUS?, Bill Lovick, Victory Assembly of God Church, P. O. Box 2768, Beaumont, Texas 77704.

[2]MORE THAN CONQUERORS, Terry Mize, Harrison House, P. O. Box 35035, Tulsa, Oklahoma 74135 - 1979.